From Bondage to Blessing

Discovering Our Identity in God

Jessica hintz

United States
2024

Imprint

Book Title: From Bondage to Blessing - Discovering Our Identity in God
Author: Jessica Hintz

Author: Jessica Hintz
Contact: boxingboy898337@gmail.com

CONTENTS

Introduction

In the opening of his profound letter to the Galatians, Paul boldly confronts the enemies of Grace, a battle he has fought throughout this remarkable first volume of his work. His journey as an apostle has not been without pain; he has suffered extensively at the hands of both Jews and Gentiles who reject the radical message of grace that he preaches. With deep concern for his followers, Paul is determined not to let them slip back into the rigid traditions of Judaism, even though some of his most fervent converts were drawn from that very faith. It is this tension that fuels his passionate critique of the notion that one can add to the pure gospel of Christ with legalistic practices and beliefs.

Paul's writing serves as a powerful reminder that the essence of the gospel lies not in adherence to the law but in the unmerited favor of God—grace. This central theme resonates throughout the epistle, as Paul lays down guidelines that apply not only to the Judaizers of his day but also to the myriad ways in which humanity continues to distort the true gospel. His message remains strikingly relevant today, where similar errors can be observed, often manifesting as a dangerous mix of faith and works.

Grace and Law: Grace vs. Law

Paul begins his defense by establishing the unmistakable authority of Christ as the source of salvation. In Galatians 1:5, he highlights the significance of the grace that comes through Jesus, emphasizing that it is this grace alone that can liberate humanity from the evil of the present age, which includes the oppressive structures set up by misguided religious leaders. His fierce opposition to the Judaizers—a group that sought to impose Jewish laws on Gentile believers—comes into sharp focus as he launches a fervent attack against them.

In Galatians 1:6-7, Paul expresses his astonishment at the Galatians' readiness to abandon the grace of Christ for what he calls "a different gospel." He writes, "I am amazed that you are turning away from Him who called you by the grace of Christ to a different gospel, which is not another; but there are some who trouble you and want to pervert the gospel of Christ." This statement encapsulates the urgency of his message: there is no alternative to the grace that Jesus offers. Any deviation from this grace constitutes a betrayal of the very foundation of Christian faith.

The Process of Turning Away

The phrase Paul uses, "you are (in the middle of) turning away," carries profound implications. It suggests a process—a journey in the wrong direction that has not yet reached its destination. The Galatians are not merely making a one-time mistake; they are engaged in a gradual drifting away from the truth. This process can be likened to a ship slowly veering off course, unaware of the dangers that lie ahead. The rationale of the flesh, driven by human reasoning and societal pressures, has blinded them to the truth. Instead of relying on the discernment of the Spirit, they are teetering on the brink of spiritual disaster.

Paul's use of the term *metastrepho* (Greek: μεταστρέφω) highlights the nature of this transformation—corruption rather than sanctification. The term conveys a sense of turning across or changing into something else. It signifies a distortion, a metamorphosis into a version of the gospel that is no longer recognizable. Paul's choice of words is deliberate; he wants the Galatians to understand the gravity of their situation. They are not just drifting away; they are in the process of being corrupted, of turning the truth of Christ into a falsehood.

The Judaizers and Their Legacy

As Paul reflects on the Judaizers of his day, he draws attention to a pattern that has persisted throughout history. The temptation to blend the gospel of grace with legalistic practices is as old as the faith itself. Just as the Judaizers sought to impose circumcision and adherence to the law on new believers, modern-day movements often introduce additional requirements for salvation—be it rituals, moral codes, or extra-biblical traditions. The ease with which people adopt these untrue versions of Christ remains alarming.

Today, we witness various forms of apostasy—individuals and groups who have once embraced the gospel but have since turned away to follow a diluted version of Christianity. These movements often begin with good intentions, aiming to make faith more relevant or accessible. However, as history shows, the path of compromise can lead to a dangerous deviation from the truth. Paul's warning resonates powerfully in this context, reminding us of the imperative to guard the purity of the gospel against any and all distortions.

The Call to Discernment

The need for discernment in the faith community is more crucial than ever. The Galatians, like many today, were caught in a web of conflicting messages. The allure of a more comfortable faith—one that promises approval through works rather than grace—can be tempting. It is essential for believers to ground themselves in the truth of the Word of God and to cultivate a relationship with the Holy Spirit, who provides guidance and wisdom in navigating these complexities.

Paul's exhortation is not merely a historical critique but a timeless call to action. He urges the Galatians—and by extension, all of us—to remain vigilant, to recognize the signs of spiritual drifting, and to reject any notion that undermines the sufficiency of Christ's sacrifice. The stakes are high; the gospel is at risk of being perverted, and with it, the very essence of faith itself.

Abandoning God God (the Father) who created them to be a sinful act. God has been the God who brought the people (and us) to"the "grace of Christ" in the first place. This is at the core of gospel preaching. This is the goal in the evangelism process. The Apostle's call is to do this. The prophet's response and the pastor's primary message, and the teacher's frame. If it is corrupted by the gospel it corrupts and influences all the ministries of the grace ministry and impedes gospel grace into an unbelievers world (Gentile) and is lost!

Conclusion

In confronting the enemies of Grace, Paul sets forth a clarion call to uphold the true gospel of Christ. His passionate defense serves as both a warning and an encouragement for believers across generations. The struggle against legalism and the temptation to add to the gospel continues to this day, and Paul's words provide a roadmap for discerning the authentic message of grace.

As we reflect on this powerful message, let us commit ourselves to the pursuit of truth. Let us be vigilant against the allure of false teachings and the subtle compromises that threaten to dilute our faith. In a world rife with confusion and spiritual turmoil, we must hold fast to the gospel of grace, allowing it to transform our lives and guide our actions. Paul's letter to the Galatians reminds us that our hope lies not in the law but in the unchanging grace of Christ, a grace that calls us to live in freedom and to share that freedom with others.

WE ARE SAVED BY THE GRACE OF GOD—NOTHING MORE!

At the very core of the Christian faith lies a fundamental truth that Paul emphasized time and again: we are saved by the grace of God—nothing more, nothing less. This profound declaration encapsulates the heart of the gospel, distinguishing it from every other religious system that seeks to establish a relationship with God through human effort or adherence to the law. It is the liberating message that affirms that salvation is not earned through works or rituals, but rather, it is a free gift bestowed upon us by a loving God who desires relationship over legalism.

Despite this clear message of grace, Paul faced an alarming challenge among the Galatian Christians. Some members from Jewish conversions, alongside those who maintained strict adherence to Jewish religious customs, were advocating that these new believers observe the Mosaic Law and practice circumcision as essential components of their faith. This pressure to conform to the law not only threatened the freedom that the gospel of grace provides but also sought to undermine the transformative work of Christ in the lives of the Galatian believers.

Such insistence on legalistic practices was not merely a minor disagreement; it was an outright assault on the very essence of Paul's ministry. For Paul, the implications were profound. He viewed this as an attack not just on the Jerusalem church, which had been a focal point of the early Christian community, but more significantly as an assault on the doctrine he had painstakingly established. His entire ministry was rooted in the belief that salvation comes solely through faith in Christ, and any attempt to add to that was a direct challenge to the message he preached.

Paul's response was fierce and unwavering. He was not a man to sit back and allow such heresies to gain traction within the church. He understood that even the slightest compromise could lead to a slippery slope, where one deviation from the truth could snowball into widespread confusion and error. This awareness compelled him to take immediate action; he was unwilling to let the matter "slide" or simply hope that it would resolve itself over time. The stakes were too high, and he recognized that allowing false teachings to take root could have catastrophic consequences for the body of Christ.

This concern raises an important question for the modern church: are we witnessing similar patterns today? Are we, as a community of believers, accepting errors that could establish an irreversible status quo among believers? The parallels between Paul's time and our own are striking. Just as the early church grappled with the influences of legalism and the pressure to conform to certain practices, today's church often finds itself navigating similar challenges.

In Galatians 5:7-11, Paul poses a rhetorical question that cuts to the heart of the issue: "Who has stopped you from pursuing the truth?" He emphasizes that the persuasion leading them away from grace does not originate from the One who called them. Here, Paul uses the metaphor of leaven to illustrate how even a tiny amount of false teaching can corrupt the entire lump of dough. His warning is clear: allowing even a small amount of legalism or compromise to enter the church can lead to significant distortions of the gospel.

Paul's confidence in the Galatians is apparent when he states, "I trust in you, and in the Lord that you will never have other thoughts." He believed in their ability to discern truth from error, anchored in their relationship with Christ. Yet, he also issued a stark warning to those who were troubling them: "anyone who is troubling you will be judged, no matter who the person is." This serves as a sobering reminder that the integrity of the gospel must be defended at all costs, and those who seek to undermine it will face consequences.

In this context, we find an important insight for the contemporary church, which is rife with "troublers." The challenge remains to recognize and address those influences that seek to dilute or distort the truth of the gospel. Just as Paul wielded the sword of the Word to confront false teachings, so too must we engage with Scripture to combat the dragons of compromise and legalism that threaten to infiltrate our communities.

Ultimately, Paul's message in Galatians serves as a timeless guide for believers today. He underscores a crucial principle: "if it doesn't start with Christ and end with Christ, it's not worthy of consideration." This declaration challenges us to evaluate every teaching, doctrine, and practice through the lens of Christ's finished work on the cross. We must remain vigilant, discerning the voices that seek to lead us away from the grace that is ours in Christ. By anchoring ourselves in the truth of the gospel, we can stand firm against the pressures of legalism and faithfully uphold the message of grace that has the power to transform lives and communities.

A Timeless Guideline for Our Time

In the landscape of modern Christianity, where the essence of the gospel is often obscured by various distractions, the words of the Apostle Paul serve as a vital guideline for the present time. His fierce commitment to the message of grace stands in stark contrast to the legalism that threatens to infiltrate the church. Paul's epistle to the Galatians is not just an ancient letter; it is a clarion call for believers to hold fast to the true gospel—the gospel that centers on the grace of God and the redemptive work of Jesus Christ.

Paul's insistence on the purity of the gospel is underscored by a particularly strong invective found in Galatians 1:8-9: "But even if we, or an angel from heaven, preach any other gospel to you than what we have preached to you, let him be accursed. As we have said before, so now I say again, if anyone preaches any other gospel to you than what you have received, let him be accursed." Here, Paul establishes a serious tone. He is emphatic that any deviation from the gospel he preached is not just a minor infraction but a grave error deserving of condemnation.

THE GRAVITY OF DISTORTION

Paul's language is intentional; he uses the word "accursed" to signify a complete and utter rejection of any teaching that contradicts the gospel of grace. This is not a mere theological disagreement; it is a matter of life and death—spiritually speaking. The stakes are incredibly high because the integrity of the gospel is at risk. Paul understands that introducing a different gospel undermines the very foundation of salvation that Jesus Christ established through His sacrificial death on the cross.

His urgency is palpable when he states that even if an angel from heaven were to proclaim a different gospel, that angel would be deserving of the same curse. This declaration serves as a powerful reminder that our source of truth must always be grounded in Christ and the revelation He provided through His apostles. Paul makes it clear that human and angelic authority cannot supersede the truth of the gospel. Any teaching that seeks to add to or distort the gospel is to be rejected outright.

The New Law in Christ

Paul goes on to articulate a crucial theological concept: Jesus Christ gave His life to free humanity from the curse imposed by the Law. This brings forth a critical understanding of grace—the realization that we are no longer bound by the constraints of the Mosaic Law but are liberated by the Law of Grace. In Christ, a new law emerges, one that is founded on grace, not on human effort or adherence to the law.

In Galatians 1:15-16, Paul shares his testimony of how he was called by God's grace, emphasizing that his salvation was not a result of human initiative or merit. He writes, "But when it pleased God, who separated me from my mother's womb and called me through His grace, to reveal His Son in me, that I might preach Him among the Gentiles." This passage is deeply significant, as it underscores that Paul's calling and mission were entirely the work of God's grace.

Paul's Identity as a Minister of Grace

Paul identifies himself as a minister of grace, one who is appointed by grace and sustained by grace. This self-identification is more than just a title; it reflects the very core of his ministry. He recognizes that grace is not only the means of his salvation but also the foundation of his calling. This acknowledgment is critical because it positions Paul as a servant of the gospel, whose mission is to proclaim the unadulterated truth of Christ's work on the cross.

Reflecting on this declaration reveals a stark reality about modern ministry. Many contemporary ministers struggle to articulate their calling in terms of grace. They often become entangled in the performance-driven aspects of ministry, prioritizing metrics of success over the transformative power of grace. This disconnect leads to a profound misunderstanding of what it means to be a minister of the gospel, resulting in a dilution of the message.

The implications of this are significant: when ministers lack a clear understanding of grace, their congregations are left without the tools necessary to recognize and combat false teachings. The lives of countless individuals are adversely affected when the grace of God is not affirmed and celebrated within the church. Paul's insistence on the centrality of grace is not merely a theological position; it is a pastoral concern that seeks to safeguard the faith of the community.

A Call to Action

Paul could not stand idly by while false teachings threatened the integrity of the gospel. He understood that the situation was dire, and he felt a profound responsibility to address it head-on. Just as Paul engaged in this spiritual battle, we, too, must take up the mantle of defending the gospel against any distortions that may arise within our churches today. It is imperative that we do not allow the message of grace to be compromised or diminished.

In the midst of this battle, Paul asserts his divine credentials, emphasizing that his authority to preach the gospel is not derived from human connections or the approval of others. He writes about how he did not consult with flesh and blood but received direct revelation from God. Paul's confidence in his calling and mission is unshakeable; he knows that his instructions come from God alone.

This conviction is powerfully illustrated through his account of encountering the Judaizers—those who sought to impose the Law on new converts. Paul recounts the story of Titus, a Greek believer who was working alongside him in ministry. Titus had not been circumcised, and this raised significant questions among the Jewish believers regarding his legitimacy as a minister of the gospel. The Judaizers challenged Paul's decision to allow Titus to travel with him, insisting that adherence to the Law was necessary for acceptance within the community of faith.

THE CHALLENGE OF LEGALISM

The confrontation surrounding Titus serves as a poignant reminder of the pervasive nature of legalism, even within the early church. The question of whether Titus could serve and minister in his "uncircumcised" state highlights the struggle between the freedom found in grace and the bondage of the Law. For the Judaizers, the external markers of faith, such as circumcision, were paramount. However, Paul's perspective was radically different; he understood that true faith is evidenced not by external compliance to the Law but by an internal transformation brought about by the grace of God.

In defending Titus, Paul underscores the core message of the gospel: that salvation and acceptance before God are based on faith in Christ, not on adherence to the Law. He contends that requiring circumcision as a prerequisite for fellowship contradicts the very essence of the grace that Jesus offers. Paul's stance is a bold declaration of the freedom believers have in Christ, a freedom that liberates them from the shackles of legalism.

THE IMPORTANCE OF UPHOLDING GRACE

As we reflect on Paul's powerful testimony and his unwavering commitment to the message of grace, we are reminded of our own responsibilities as believers. The current church must remain vigilant against the subtle encroachments of legalism and false teachings that can lead to spiritual bondage. It is essential that we uphold the truth of the gospel and ensure that grace remains central to our understanding of faith and ministry.

Paul's journey and his fierce advocacy for the gospel of grace compel us to evaluate our own understanding of grace and its role in our lives. Are we truly embracing the transformative power of grace in our personal walk with Christ? Are we proclaiming this message to others, and are we nurturing communities that reflect the grace of God? The answers to these questions will determine the health and vitality of our faith and the effectiveness of our ministry.

In a world filled with competing ideologies and distractions, let us heed Paul's call to remain steadfast in the grace that is ours in Christ Jesus. Just as Paul fought tirelessly to preserve the purity of the gospel, we too must take up the mantle of defending this sacred message, ensuring that it continues to transform lives and draw people into a relationship with the living God. The gospel of grace is not merely a doctrine to be taught; it is a reality to be lived out, reflecting the love and mercy of God to a world in desperate need of hope.

Paul's Astonishment and the Judaizers

Paul was astonished. His surprise wasn't merely a reaction to the unusual nature of the Galatians' behavior; it stemmed from a profound disappointment that the very people he had worked diligently to minister to were entertaining false teachings and deviating from the gospel of grace. In his letter, Paul scolds the Galatians with a rhetorical question: "Who are these guys?" He refers to the Judaizers, a group of individuals who were pushing a legalistic agenda, insisting that adherence to the Law and practices like circumcision were necessary for salvation. "How then could you Galatians entertain them, even allowing some of yours to follow their doctrine?" Paul's incredulity is palpable, and it resonates with questions we might ask ourselves today.

Paul's strong reaction reveals not just his personal feelings but a critical understanding of the implications these false teachings have for the gospel. In Galatians 2:5-6, he writes, "We did not yield in submission even for a moment, so that the truth of the gospel might be preserved for you. And from those who seemed to be influential, what they were makes no difference to me; God shows no partiality." Here, Paul emphasizes the importance of maintaining the integrity of the gospel, regardless of the status or perceived authority of those spreading false teachings. His commitment to truth is unwavering, reflecting a profound understanding that the gospel is not contingent upon human approval or tradition.

The Nature of Paul's Ministry

Paul's ministry was characterized by a clear distinction between the message of grace and the demands of the Law. While he acknowledged that Peter and other apostles had specific missions to the Jewish people, he remained resolute in his calling to the Gentiles. This distinction highlights a broader theme within the New Testament: that the gospel transcends cultural and religious boundaries. Paul's mission was not defined by the Law but by the grace of God, which was available to all people.

The early church had reached a consensus at the Jerusalem Council, agreeing that non-Jewish believers should not be burdened with the requirements of the Law, such as circumcision. Instead, they were only instructed to avoid certain practices to foster unity among believers. This decision underscored a fundamental truth: the Law served as a temporary guide, a tutor that pointed to Christ. As Paul articulates in Galatians 3:24-25, "So the law was our guardian until Christ came, that we might be justified by faith. Now that this faith has come, we are no longer under a guardian." The transition from law to grace signifies a shift in how believers relate to God—a relationship grounded in faith rather than works.

Paul's Theological Argument

The implications of this shift are profound. Paul is not just defending his ministry; he is laying the groundwork for understanding the very nature of salvation. In Galatians 2:20, he shares a verse that has become a cornerstone of Christian identity: "I have been crucified with Christ, and I no longer live, but Christ lives in me. The life I now live in the body, I live by faith in the Son of God, who loved me and gave himself for me." This declaration encapsulates the essence of the Christian life: it is not about adhering to a set of rules or traditions but about living in relationship with Christ, empowered by His grace.

Paul's firm stance against the Judaizers illustrates his understanding of the danger posed by those who would add conditions to the gospel. He draws a clear line of demarcation, stating that if the Galatians sided with the Judaizers, they would be severing themselves from the grace that is found in Christ. In Galatians 2:21, he asserts, "I do not set aside the grace of God, for if righteousness could be gained through the law, Christ died for nothing!" This statement serves as a powerful reminder that any attempt to earn salvation through works undermines the very foundation of the gospel.

The Bewitchment of the Galatians

Paul's frustration reaches a peak when he addresses the Galatians with the exclamation, "O foolish Galatians! Who has bewitched you?" This rhetorical question captures the essence of his concern: how could they so quickly abandon the truth of the gospel for a distorted version? By invoking the term "bewitched," Paul highlights the spiritual deception at play, equating the influence of the Judaizers with witchcraft. This accusation is both alarming and sobering, as it suggests that the Galatians are under a powerful spell, one that clouds their judgment and leads them away from the truth.

At the heart of the Judaizers' argument was a claim to lineage, asserting, "We are Abraham's seed." Paul counters this by emphasizing the nature of the promise given to Abraham, explaining that it is not genealogy that grants righteousness but faith. In Galatians 3:24-29, he elaborates on this idea: "So in Christ Jesus you are all children of God through faith… if you belong to Christ, then you are Abraham's seed, and heirs according to the promise." Paul effectively dismantles the Judaizers' arguments by shifting the focus from ethnic identity to spiritual identity in Christ.

Paul's Fear for the Galatians

Amidst his theological arguments, Paul expresses his deep concern for the Galatians. In Galatians 4:9-11, he states, "But now that you have come to know God, or rather to be known by God, how can you turn back again to the weak and worthless elementary principles of the world, whose slaves you want to be once more? You observe days and months and seasons and years! I am afraid I may have labored over you in vain." His fear is not simply about their spiritual well-being but also about the potential loss of what he worked tirelessly to establish among them. This fear echoes through the centuries as a reminder of the dangers of falling back into legalism and ritualism.

Paul's rhetorical questions challenge the Galatians to consider the implications of their choices. Having experienced the freedom and grace of God, why would they want to return to the constraints of the Law? The juxtaposition of knowing God and returning to "weak and worthless" principles serves as a stark warning against complacency and regression in faith. His words urge us to examine our own lives and identify areas where we may unwittingly revert to a performance-based understanding of our relationship with God.

The Nature of False Teaching

In Galatians 4:16-17, Paul confronts the motivations of those who sought to sway the Galatians away from the truth. "Have I then become your enemy by telling you the truth? They make much of you, but for no good purpose. They want to exclude you, that you may make much of them." Paul recognizes that the false teachers are not interested in the spiritual growth of the Galatians; rather, they seek to manipulate and control them for their own gain. This insight remains relevant in today's church, where some leaders may promote their agendas at the expense of the gospel.

Paul's clarity about the nature of false teaching is vital for the church today. Just as he discerned the motivations behind the Judaizers, we too must be vigilant in recognizing voices that lead us away from the truth. It is essential to evaluate teachings against the standard of Scripture and the gospel of grace. Any teaching that distorts the message of grace or seeks to impose additional burdens on believers should be met with caution and, if necessary, rejection.

The Danger of Falling from Grace

In Galatians 5:4, Paul provides a sobering warning: "You are severed from Christ, you who would be justified by the law; you have fallen away from grace." The fall from grace is not merely a theological concept; it signifies a profound spiritual crisis. When individuals or communities turn away from the gospel and attempt to attain righteousness through their efforts, they effectively cut themselves off from the very source of their salvation.

Paul's words serve as a stark reminder that grace is not something to be taken for granted. It is essential to recognize that departing from grace is a serious matter with eternal consequences. As believers, we must remain steadfast in the freedom that Christ offers, resisting the temptation to revert to legalistic practices or performance-based faith.

The Law of Liberty

In Galatians 5:1, Paul exhorts the Galatians, "For freedom Christ has set us free; stand firm therefore, and do not submit again to a yoke of slavery." This call to freedom is central to the message of the New Testament. Paul emphasizes that the grace of God ushers in a new paradigm—a law of liberty that liberates believers from the constraints of the Law. The freedom that Christ offers is not a license to sin but an invitation to live in relationship with Him, empowered by the Holy Spirit.

The law of liberty is a transformative reality for those who place their faith in Christ. It signifies the release from the burdens of the Law and the embrace of a life defined by grace. This freedom allows believers to live authentically, guided by the Spirit rather than by the demands of a legalistic framework. Paul's passionate plea for the Galatians to embrace this freedom is a call to all believers to recognize the depth of God's grace and the implications it has for their lives.

A Call to Vigilance

In conclusion, Paul's message to the Galatians remains profoundly relevant today. His astonishment at their willingness to entertain false teachings serves as a cautionary tale for the contemporary church. As we navigate a world filled with competing ideologies and teachings, we must remain vigilant in upholding the truth of the gospel. The call to embrace grace, resist legalism, and live in the freedom of Christ is as urgent now as it was in Paul's time.

THE DECLARATION OF INDEPENDENCE IN FAITH

The epistle to the Galatians is a powerful manifesto of freedom—a "declaration of independence" for all who believe in Christ. Paul passionately defends the notion that faith in Jesus liberates believers from the bondage of sin and the legalistic constraints of the Law. This message resonates throughout the letter, providing not just theological principles but practical guidelines for living a life empowered by grace.

Paul's insistence that believers should not be ensnared by sin is central to his message. He lays out a vivid portrayal of the consequences of indulging in sinful behavior. In Galatians 5:19-21, he enumerates a list of acts that lead to spiritual bondage: sexual immorality, idolatry, hatred, discord, jealousy, and more. His conclusion is stark and uncompromising: "Those who practice such things will not inherit the kingdom of God." This declaration serves as both a warning and a call to holiness, urging believers to pursue a lifestyle that reflects their new identity in Christ.

Walking in the Spirit

The antidote to the desires of the flesh, Paul asserts, is found in walking in the Spirit. In Galatians 5:16, he exhorts the Galatians, "Walk by the Spirit, and you will not gratify the desires of the flesh." This call to walk in the Spirit introduces a transformative concept: the empowerment of the believer through the Holy Spirit. Walking in the Spirit is not merely a metaphorical journey; it represents a profound relational dynamic where the believer is guided and strengthened by the Spirit of God.

Paul further elaborates on how grace manifests in practical action. In Galatians 5:13, he emphasizes that while believers are called to liberty, they should not use this freedom as an excuse to indulge in selfish desires. Instead, they are to serve one another in love. This radical reorientation from self-serving to others-focused is the essence of a life lived in the Spirit.

The Fruits of the Spirit

Galatians 5:22-23 introduces the concept of the "fruits of the Spirit," which serve as a litmus test for the authenticity of one's spiritual walk. Paul lists these fruits: love, joy, peace, patience, kindness, goodness, faithfulness, gentleness, and self-control. Each of these characteristics represents the active work of the Holy Spirit in the life of a believer, transforming their nature and guiding their actions.

This transformation is not merely internal; it has external implications. A life marked by the fruits of the Spirit is a life that builds up the community, fosters genuine relationships, and reflects the character of Christ. In contrast to the acts of the flesh, which lead to division and strife, the fruits of the Spirit cultivate unity and harmony among believers.

Paul's vision for the church is one where grace reigns, and the Spirit guides every interaction. He encourages the Galatians to focus on living out these fruits, reminding them that there is no law against such things. In other words, these qualities fulfill the intent of the Law, which is to promote love and righteousness among God's people.

The Burden of Community

Central to Paul's message in Galatians is the theme of community and mutual support. In Galatians 6:1-2, he writes, "Brothers, if anyone is caught in any transgression, you who are spiritual should restore him in a spirit of gentleness." This instruction highlights the importance of a grace-filled approach to dealing with sin within the community of believers. Rather than casting judgment or ostracizing those who fall, Paul calls for restoration and gentle correction.

He underscores the necessity of bearing one another's burdens as a fulfillment of the law of Christ. This principle of burden-bearing is critical to the life of the church. It fosters an environment of grace where individuals feel safe to confess struggles and seek help without fear of condemnation. The body of Christ is meant to be a refuge, a place where healing and restoration can occur.

Paul's emphasis on community also reflects the reality of the human experience. No one is immune to struggles, failures, or sin. The call to bear one another's burdens is an acknowledgment that we are stronger together, leaning on each other for support and encouragement as we navigate the challenges of life.

The Danger of Self-Righteousness

In contrast to the grace-filled community Paul envisions, he warns against self-righteousness and judgmental attitudes that often arise in religious circles. The tendency to point fingers and heap condemnation on those who falter is a trap that the church must avoid. Paul's critique of the Judaizers serves as a caution against a graceless ministry that focuses on outward appearances and legalistic adherence to rules rather than genuine faith and love.

He highlights the hypocrisy of those who seek to impose burdens on others while neglecting their own failings. This self-righteous attitude is contrary to the very heart of the gospel. Instead of fostering an environment of grace, it creates division and alienation. Paul's admonition to restore gently and bear one another's burdens counters this tendency, promoting a culture of humility and compassion.

The Importance of Personal Responsibility

Interestingly, in Galatians 6:5, Paul asserts, "For each will have to bear his own load." While the church community is called to support one another, personal responsibility is also paramount. Each believer is accountable for their own actions and spiritual growth. This dual emphasis on community and individual responsibility ensures that while we uplift one another, we also recognize our personal journey of faith.

Bearing one's own load implies an active engagement in one's spiritual life. It is a call to maturity, where believers are encouraged to take ownership of their relationship with Christ. This balance between collective support and individual accountability is essential for a healthy church community.

Grace in Action

As Paul concludes this epistle, he underscores the importance of living out grace in action. In Galatians 6:7-8, he warns, "Do not be deceived: God is not mocked, for whatever one sows, that will he also reap." This principle of sowing and reaping applies to both spiritual and practical aspects of life. If we sow into the flesh—by indulging in sin and self-serving behavior—we will reap the consequences. Conversely, if we sow into the Spirit—by living in alignment with God's will and serving others—we will reap eternal life and blessings.

Paul's call to action is clear: grace must be an active force in our lives. It should compel us to do good to everyone, especially those within the household of faith. This ministry of grace is not a passive endeavor; it requires intentionality and effort. We are called to be vessels of grace, extending kindness, love, and support to those around us.

Final Reflections on Paul's Message

As Paul concludes his letter to the Galatians, he reaffirms the transformative power of the gospel. He emphasizes that in Christ, neither circumcision nor uncircumcision has any value; what counts is a new creation (Galatians 6:15). This declaration encapsulates the heart of the gospel message: that our identity is found in Christ alone, not in our adherence to religious rules or cultural norms.

The closing verses of Galatians reflect Paul's deep concern for the Galatians and his desire for them to embrace the true essence of the gospel. He encourages them to focus on the grace of Jesus Christ, which is the foundation for their faith and the source of their strength. In this grace, there is peace, hope, and a sense of belonging.

CONCLUSION

In summary, Paul's epistle to the Galatians serves as a powerful reminder of the freedom we have in Christ. His declaration of independence from sin and legalism invites us to embrace a life of grace, characterized by the fruits of the Spirit and a commitment to community. The challenges of self-righteousness, judgment, and apathy are countered by a call to bear one another's burdens and walk in the Spirit.

As we reflect on this message, let us consider how we can embody the principles of grace in our lives and in our communities. Are we actively walking in the Spirit, seeking to bear one another's burdens, and extending grace to those around us? Paul's words encourage us to live out our faith authentically, demonstrating the love of Christ to a world in need. May we strive to be vessels of grace, reflecting the heart of Jesus in all we do.

THE FOUNDATION OF FAITH: UNDERSTANDING THE GOSPEL OF GRACE THROUGH REVELATION

In the heart of Christian theology lies the essential doctrine of grace—a truth that transforms lives and shapes ministries. The epistle to the Galatians, penned by the Apostle Paul, serves as a cornerstone for understanding the gospel of grace as received through divine revelation. In a world often characterized by confusion and misunderstanding, it is vital to have a clear vision of the foundation upon which one is built in order to engage in authentic preaching and effective ministry.

THE ROLE OF REVELATION

Paul's assertion in **Galatians 1:11-12** is unequivocal: "For I would have you know, brethren, that the gospel which was preached by me is not according to man. For I neither received it from man, nor was I taught it, but it came through the revelation of Jesus Christ." This passage underscores a critical point: the gospel is not a product of human ingenuity or tradition. It is a divine revelation, a truth that originates from God Himself. Without this understanding, any attempt at ministry will lack the authenticity and authority that come from a genuine encounter with the divine.

The foundation of our faith must be rooted in revelation. Paul's own experience of solitude in the wilderness, where he sought the Lord fervently, exemplifies the necessity of seeking God above all else. Rather than relying on human teachings or traditions, he prioritized direct communion with God, which ultimately shaped his theology and ministry. This principle is essential for contemporary ministers as well; they must seek the face of God in order to accurately convey His truths to the congregation.

The Power of Revelation in Ministry

Paul's ministry was governed by revelation, as demonstrated in **Galatians 2:1-2**: "Then after fourteen years, I went up again to Jerusalem with Barnabas and took Titus with me. And I went up by revelation and communicated to them that gospel which I preach among the Gentiles." Here, Paul indicates that his mission was not simply a response to the needs of the people or the traditions of the church; it was a divine appointment. This underscores a profound truth: effective ministry arises from a clear understanding of God's calling and direction.

In the early days of the church, leaders often received revelations that guided their decisions and actions. One notable example is the ministry of Clayt Sonmore, who played a pivotal role in the Full Gospel Businessmen's Meetings. Through divine revelation, issues of sin and hidden agendas among leaders were brought to light, prompting necessary corrections and leading to a flourishing of faith and practice. This model of ministry, grounded in the work of the Holy Spirit, is a stark contrast to the often superficial approaches seen in many contemporary churches today.

Confronting Hypocrisy

In **Galatians 2:11-14**, Paul confronts Peter regarding his hypocrisy in Antioch: "But when Peter came to Antioch, I opposed him to his face, because he stood condemned. For before certain men came from James, he used to eat with the Gentiles; but when they came, he drew back and separated himself, fearing the circumcision party." This confrontation is crucial, as it illustrates Paul's commitment to the truth of the gospel. Paul was not afraid to challenge even the most prominent leaders when their actions contradicted the principles of the faith.

Today, there seems to be a reluctance within many church circles to address issues of hypocrisy and immorality among leaders. The silence on such matters can lead to a culture of complacency and apathy, where truth is sacrificed for the sake of maintaining relationships or appearances. Paul's example challenges modern leaders to uphold the integrity of the gospel, regardless of the potential fallout. He demonstrates that true love for the church necessitates a willingness to confront sin, regardless of the cost.

The Spirit's Work in the Church

In **Galatians 3:5**, Paul raises an important question regarding the role of the Holy Spirit in the life of the church: "Does he who supplies the Spirit to you and works miracles among you do so by works of the law, or by hearing with faith?" Here, Paul emphasizes that the presence and power of the Holy Spirit are not contingent upon adherence to the Law but are accessed through faith. This principle is crucial for understanding the nature of God's work in the lives of believers.

The contemporary church often experiences a disconnect between the power of the Spirit and the day-to-day ministry. The lack of miracles and manifestations of the Spirit's power can often be attributed to a diminished expectation or a focus on human effort rather than divine intervention. In mission fields, however, the evidence of the Spirit's work is undeniable. Reports of miraculous healings, resurrections, and explosive growth in congregations serve as a reminder that where the Holy Spirit is honored and sought, powerful things can happen.

THE BLESSINGS OF ABRAHAM

Paul elaborates on the blessings conferred to believers through faith in **Galatians 3:6-9**: "Just as Abraham 'believed God, and it was counted to him as righteousness,' know then that it is those of faith who are the sons of Abraham." This foundational truth underscores the continuity of God's promises from the Old Testament to the New Testament. The blessings promised to Abraham extend to all who put their faith in Christ, regardless of their ethnic or cultural background.

Furthermore, Paul argues that the inheritance granted to believers is not based on lineage or adherence to the Law, but on faith in Jesus Christ. **Galatians 3:13-14** states, "Christ redeemed us from the curse of the law by becoming a curse for us—for it is written, 'Cursed is everyone who is hanged on a tree'—so that in Christ Jesus the blessing of Abraham might come to the Gentiles." This radical inclusion emphasizes that salvation and blessings are available to all who believe, breaking down barriers that once divided people.

The Theology of Inclusion

Paul's teachings in **Galatians 3:26-29** further reinforce the theology of inclusion: "For in Christ Jesus you are all sons of God, through faith. For as many of you as were baptized into Christ have put on Christ. There is neither Jew nor Greek, slave nor free, male nor female, for you are all one in Christ Jesus." This profound declaration shatters social and cultural barriers, promoting a radical unity among believers. In Christ, distinctions that once held significant weight become irrelevant.

This message remains vitally relevant today, as the church grapples with issues of division and inequality. Paul's insistence on the equality of all believers in Christ challenges churches to reflect the inclusivity of the gospel in their practices and attitudes. It invites the body of Christ to embrace diversity, recognizing that all are equal heirs of the promises of God.

The Promise of the Holy Spirit

In **Ephesians 1:13-14**, Paul elaborates on the role of the Holy Spirit as a seal of the believer's inheritance: "In him you also, when you heard the word of truth, the gospel of your salvation, and believed in him, were sealed with the promised Holy Spirit, who is the guarantee of our inheritance until we acquire possession of it, to the praise of his glory." This sealing of the Holy Spirit is a powerful assurance for believers, affirming that they belong to God and are part of His eternal plan.

The Holy Spirit not only empowers believers for ministry but also serves as a reminder of the hope and future inheritance awaiting them. This understanding should embolden believers to live out their faith with confidence and purpose, knowing they are equipped by the Spirit to carry out God's mission in the world.

Conclusion: The Call to Authenticity

The teachings found in Galatians and Ephesians call the church to return to its roots—a return to a gospel grounded in revelation, empowered by the Holy Spirit, and characterized by grace. The authentic preaching of the gospel requires a clear understanding of its foundations, rooted in personal revelation and faith. It challenges contemporary leaders to rise above complacency, confronting hypocrisy and fostering a culture of accountability within the church.

Moreover, as we reflect on the blessings of Abraham and the inclusive nature of the gospel, we are reminded of our responsibility to create communities that embrace and celebrate diversity. The call to authentic ministry is a call to reflect the heart of Christ, reaching out to all, regardless of their background.

In a world in desperate need of hope, the gospel of grace remains our greatest message. As believers, we are tasked with carrying this message to the ends of the earth, empowered by the Spirit and guided by revelation. Let us strive to be faithful stewards of this incredible gift, living out our faith authentically and boldly proclaiming the truth of the gospel to all who will hear.

THE SONS AND DAUGHTERS OF GOD: UNDERSTANDING OUR IDENTITY IN THE FINAL DAYS

In the final days, the sons and daughters of God will be fully revealed, showcasing their identity and purpose as heirs to the divine promise. This identity is deeply rooted in the understanding of being "sons of freeborn" as opposed to the "sons of bondwomen." In this discourse, we will explore the implications of this distinction, the historical context surrounding it, and its relevance to contemporary faith communities.

SONS OF FREEBORN: A BIBLICAL FOUNDATION

The Apostle Paul provides a profound explanation of our identity in **Galatians 4:30-31**, where he states, "But what does the Scripture say? 'Cast out the bondwoman and her son; for the son of the bondwoman shall not be heir with the son of the freewoman.' So then, brethren, we are not children of the bondwoman but of the free." This passage draws a stark line between two kinds of offspring: those born into bondage and those born into freedom.

Paul's reference to the "bondwoman" and "freewoman" is a direct allusion to the Old Testament account of Abraham, Sarah, and Hagar. Abraham had two sons: Ishmael, born of Hagar, the bondwoman, and Isaac, born of Sarah, the freewoman. According to Scripture, the promised inheritance and covenant blessings were to flow through Isaac, not Ishmael. This critical distinction underscores the foundation of Christian identity—believers are not children of bondage but children of promise and freedom.

THE SIGNIFICANCE OF FREEDOM

The concept of being "freeborn" resonates deeply within the Christian faith. To be freeborn means to inherit the promises of God without the burdens of the Law or the shackles of sin. It signifies a relationship with God that is based on grace, not merit. This freedom is encapsulated in the work of Christ, who liberated believers from the curse of the Law by His sacrificial death and resurrection.

In a world that often seeks to blend beliefs and compromise core doctrines, Paul's words serve as a clarion call to recognize and uphold the truth of the gospel. There is no room for negotiations with ideologies that contradict the foundational tenets of Christianity. The children of the bondwoman—the descendants of Hagar—represent not only a different lineage but a contrasting understanding of God's covenant.

The Challenges of Interfaith Relations

In today's society, the call for interfaith dialogue and cooperation is prevalent. Many church leaders advocate for unity among various religious groups, believing that such collaboration can promote social justice and peace. However, Paul's message challenges this notion. He categorically states that there is no common ground between the children of promise and the children of bondage.

Despite the goodwill of interfaith ventures, such as those promoted by notable figures like Rick Warren and Tony Blair, Christians must exercise discernment. Engaging in partnerships that dilute or compromise the core message of the gospel can lead to theological confusion and compromise. The call to "cast out the bondwoman and her son" is a call to remain true to the distinctiveness of the Christian faith.

Historical Context: Abraham and His Sons

To fully appreciate Paul's message, we must revisit the story of Abraham. The saga begins with God's promise to Abraham that he would be the father of many nations. However, when Sarah, his wife, was unable to bear children, she offered her maidservant Hagar to Abraham, leading to the birth of Ishmael. This act, born of human effort rather than divine timing, set the stage for conflict.

God later reaffirmed His promise to Abraham, declaring that Sarah would bear a son, Isaac. The tension between these two sons symbolizes the ongoing struggle between faith and works, grace and law. Ishmael represents human attempts to fulfill God's promises through self-reliance, while Isaac represents the fulfillment of God's promise through divine intervention.

This historical narrative underscores the importance of understanding our heritage as children of God. As Christians, we are heirs of the promise made to Abraham through Isaac. This inheritance is not based on our performance but on God's faithfulness. Therefore, we must hold firm to our identity and resist any attempts to compromise it for the sake of societal acceptance.

The Identity of Believers in Christ

Paul's teachings in Galatians highlight the transformative nature of faith in Christ. In **Galatians 3:26-29**, he writes, "For you are all sons of God through faith in Christ Jesus. For as many of you as were baptized into Christ have put on Christ. There is neither Jew nor Greek, slave nor free, male nor female; for you are all one in Christ Jesus. And if you are Christ's, then you are Abraham's seed, and heirs according to the promise."

This declaration speaks to the radical inclusivity of the gospel while maintaining the distinctiveness of identity. The message of Christ transcends cultural and social barriers, uniting believers as heirs of the promise made to Abraham. This unity does not erase individual identities; rather, it enriches the collective body of Christ.

The Final Revelation of God's Sons and Daughters

As we move closer to the final days, the sons and daughters of God will be revealed in their fullness. This revelation is not merely about individual identity but about the corporate expression of God's family on earth. In the face of increasing secularism and pluralism, the church is called to stand firm in its identity as children of the promise.

In **Romans 8:19**, Paul writes, "For the creation waits with eager longing for the revealing of the sons of God." This passage emphasizes the anticipation of a future time when believers will fully manifest their identity as God's children. This revelation is tied to the glory of God and serves as a testament to His faithfulness.

THE CALL TO DISTINCTION

In light of the current global religious landscape, the church must remain steadfast in its calling to uphold the truth of the gospel. The distinctions between the children of the bondwoman and the children of the freewoman are not merely historical or theological; they are practical and relevant. Engaging in partnerships that seek to blur these lines compromises the message of grace and diminishes the power of the gospel.

The call to "cast out the bondwoman" is a call to reject any theology or practice that seeks to align Christianity with ideologies contrary to the gospel. This does not mean Christians should engage in hostility or isolationism but rather approach interfaith dialogues with clarity and conviction. Believers must articulate their faith with grace, while remaining resolute in the truths they uphold.

CONCLUSION: EMBRACING OUR IDENTITY

As we reflect on our identity as sons and daughters of God, we must embrace the freedom that comes from being children of the promise. This identity shapes our relationship with God and with one another. It calls us to live in a manner that reflects the character of Christ, standing firm in our convictions while extending grace to those around us.

In the final days, the world will witness the manifestation of God's children—those who have fully embraced their identity as heirs of the promise. As believers, we are called to live in the light of this truth, boldly proclaiming the gospel and remaining steadfast in our faith.

Let us remember that our inheritance is not merely a future promise but a present reality. As we navigate a complex world, we can take comfort in knowing that we are freeborn, children of the Most High God, called to live out our identity with conviction and purpose. It is this identity that will shine brightly in the darkness, drawing others to the light of Christ and revealing the glory of God to all creation.

THE END